TALES OF HORROR

ALIENS

Jim Pipe

TALES OF HORROR
ALIENS

Acknowledgements

Copyright © 2006 *ticktock* Entertainment Ltd.

First published in Great Britain by ticktock Media Ltd.,

Unit 2, Orchard Business Centre, North Farm Road, Tunbridge Wells, Kent TN2 3XF, Great Britain.

All rights reserved. No part of this publication may be reproduced, stored in a retrieval system, or transmitted in any form or by

any means electronic, mechanical, photocopying, recording or otherwise, without prior written permission of the copyright owner.

A CIP catalogue record for this book is available from the British Library.

ISBN 1 84696 016 9 Printed in China.

Picture Credits

t=top, b=bottom, c=centre, l=left, r=right, OFC=outside front cover, OBC=outside back cover.

Amit Gogia CyberMedia Services: 24 (main pic), 25tr. Corbis: 7 (main pic). Fortean Picture Library 12bl, 2 bl. Mary Evans Picture Library: 20bl.

NASA Picture Library: 30/31 (main pic), 31tl. Rex Features: 15r, OFC. Science Photo Library: 16-17 (main pic), 19br. ShutterStock: 19bl, Mark Bond 6tl,

Stephen Coburn 22 (main pic), electricsoda 1c, 10br, Johanna Goodyear 11cl, Chris Harvey 8/9 (main pic: hands),

Alan C. Heison 13 (main pic), Stephen Inglis 22bc, Evgeny E. Kuklev 11 cr, Roman Krochuk 29 bl, Tyler Olsen 20/21 (main pic), Orla 10bc,

Styve Reineck 22/23 (main pic), Bora Ucack 8/9 (main pic: clipboard). ticktock Media image archive: 4bl, 5 (main pic), 10tl, 11bl, 14tl, 18tl, 19 (main pic),

24bl, 26/27 (main pic), 26tl, 28/29 (main pic), 28bl, 30tl.

With thanks to the Kentucky New Era for providing details of the Sutton story on pages 14-15.

Every effort has been made to trace the copyright holders and we apologize in advance for any unintentional ommissions.

We would be pleased to insert the appropriate acknowledgement in any subsequent edition of this publication.

IS ANYBODY OUT THERE?

You're driving along a quiet country lane. Suddenly a blinding light flashes in front of you. Your car's engine dies. As you stare into the darkness, shadowy figures creep from the woods. And then... your mind goes blank.

Many people say they have seen or met aliens. Some describe them as small, grey creatures with black, glassy eyes. Others say they look like hairy monsters with sharp, hungry teeth.

Our galaxy contains 100,000 million stars. Scientists believe that other life forms are probably out there, somewhere. But have aliens from outer space really visited Earth? Could they be here already?

Scientists are looking deep into space for signs of alien life. Who knows what they will find? Meanwhile, keep your eyes open. Have you ever woken up feeling that you didn't sleep in your bed last night? And what is that big silver dish doing in your neighbour's garage?

VISITORS FROM OUTER SPACE

Why are aliens here? Some reports are of dangerous aliens kidnapping people, or killing cattle and other animals. Other people describe meeting friendly aliens, such as the movie alien, ET. Are aliens just tourists? Or are they coming to warn us of disaster?

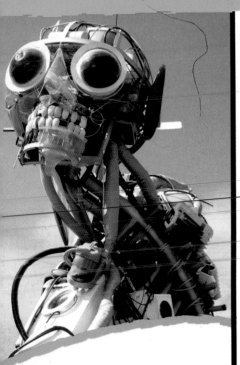

UFOs

How do aliens reach our planet from the other side of the galaxy? Most people think that spaceships, or UFOs (Unidentified Flying Objects), bring them.

Betty and Barney Hill were driving through New Hampshire, USA, in September, 1961, when they saw a UFO ahead of them. Then their minds went blank!

Later, Betty described meeting aliens on a spaceship. She had nightmares about them, too. The aliens looked human. They were just over 1.5 metres tall, and had greyish skins and 'wrap-around' eyes.

Betty drew a star map, which she says she saw on a tour of the spaceship. It showed stars in another part of our galaxy. Incredibly, this group of stars was not discovered by astronomers until eight years later!

If UFOs are able to travel through space, we won't be able to follow them very far. The fastest spacecraft made by humans is NASA's *Voyager 1*. But it is throught even *Voyager 1* would take 73,000 years to reach our nearest star (after the Sun).

SURVIVING IN SPACE

So how could aliens survive long journeys in space? Over thousands of years, their bodies would adapt to life in space.

They might find a way to 'freeze' their bodies so they do not get old on long journeys. They could also use robots to explore the universe as we do.

KINDS OF ENCOUNTERS

It's terrifying enough to see an alien spaceship landing. But thousands of people claim they have had contact with aliens or even been kidnapped by them!

In April 1964, policeman Lonnie Zamora was driving along a road in New Mexico, USA. He claimed he saw a silvery spacecraft on four legs. Two strange figures were walking near it. When the figures saw Zamora, they jumped into the craft, and took off with a roar.

A photograph taken by Zamora and his police chief show four prints on the ground from the craft's feet. There were also patches of burnt ground where it took off.

CLOSE ENCOUNTERS - 1 TO 5

Sightings of aliens or their craft are known as close encounters. There are five different types of encounter:

- **Close Encounters of the First Kind** – seeing a UFO within 100 metres or so.

- **Close Encounters of the Second Kind** – finding evidence of UFOs, such as a crop circle or signs of a UFO crash.

- **Close Encounters of the Third Kind** – seeing aliens near a UFO.

- **Close Encounters of the Fourth Kind** – being kidnapped by aliens or being taken on board an alien spacecraft.

- **Close Encounters of the Fifth Kind** – meeting with aliens or making contact with a UFO.

TYPES OF ALIEN

What do aliens look like? They can look like humans, robots, worms or giant insects. Would you like to meet one of these on a dark night?

Aliens in movies often look like animals. Some have scaly skins, like reptiles. Others behave like insects. They work in gangs to protect an egg-laying alien queen. Watch out for this type, they want to take over the world.

Aliens come in different sizes. Some are huge. Others are so tiny they worm into our bodies, and take them over. Some scientists believe that alien viruses can travel through space. Could they hitch a ride on a comet and crash land on Earth?

"They were huge round heads... This face had no nostrils... it had a pair of very large dark-coloured eyes, and just beneath this, a kind of fleshy beak. In a group round the mouth were sixteen slender, almost whip-like tentacles, arranged in two bunches of eight each."

A description of the Martians in *The War of the Worlds* (1898) by H. G. Wells.

ALIEN ABDUCTIONS

In 1957, Villa Boas, a Brazilian farmer, was dragged by aliens on to an egg-shaped spacecraft. Once on board he was stripped and covered in a strange liquid. A blood sample was taken from his chin.

Many people believe they have been taken aboard alien ships against their will. This is called alien abduction. Researchers say the following signs may show that they are telling the truth. Victims usually complain of:

- A UFO sighting.

- Nightmares about aliens; or a nagging feeling that you have met an alien.

- 'Missing time', when you cannot remember where you have been.

- Puzzling scars or burns on your body, and no memory of how they got there.

THE TRAVIS WALTON STORY

In November 1975, seven men who were working in a forest saw a UFO. One of the men, Travis Walton, went to investigate. Walton was paralysed by a beam of light from the UFO. His friends ran away thinking he was dead! Walton's body then disappeared.

Five days later, Walton turned up in a nearby town. Under hypnosis he remembered being kidnapped and examined by three tall aliens with large eyes.

UFO NESTS

Nests are outlines left wherever a UFO has landed.

In 1966, Australian Farmer George Pedley claims he saw a flying saucer lift off from a lagoon. When he went to investigate, he found a large round area of swirling water where the reeds had disappeared.

George went back to the lagoon with a friend. Amazingly, the reeds had grown back. The shape you can see in the picture is the UFO's nest.

ALIEN ATTACK

A famous Close Encounter of the Third Kind took place in August, 1955, in Kelly, Kentucky, USA.

Billy Ray Taylor was at the home of his friend Elmer Sutton when a flying saucer landed near the house.

In fear, Taylor and Sutton watched as a little man came towards the house. The alien creature had a big head, long arms with large, clawed hands and huge eyes. The friends shot at the creature. It flipped backwards, and ran off, but the gunshot did not hurt it.

For the next few hours, alien creatures surrounded the Suttons' house. They peered in windows and climbed onto the roof of the house. The terrified family tried shooting the aliens but their bullets could not harm the creatures.

Finally, Taylor and the Suttons ran to their cars, and fled to the local police station.

Afterwards, investigators tried to find evidence of the alien attack, but no sign of them was ever found.

THE ROSWELL CRASH

The disc-shaped object was half-buried in the desert. Around the craft lay four bodies. Their domed, hairless heads had round eyes and slit-like mouths. They were not human...

This famous UFO crash happened in June, 1947, outside Roswell, New Mexico, USA. A rancher called William Brazel heard an explosion during a lightning storm. The next day, he found some metal wreckage. The metal was like nothing he had ever seen on Earth. Another local man, Grady Barnett, claimed he had found a crashed UFO and four alien bodies in the same area.

The wreckage was removed by the US Air Force. A few days later, the Air Force reported that the wreckage was from a crashed weather balloon, not an alien spacecraft.

Official reports later said that there had been no UFO and no dead aliens. But many people still believe the truth was covered up.

MYSTERY BODIES AT ROSWELL

Some people say that the alien bodies from the crash at Roswell, New Mexico, were taken to a top security storage place called 'Hangar 18' at Wright Patterson Air Force Base, in Ohio, USA.

Others believe the bodies are now stored at Area 51, a secret US government base in Nevada, USA.

Were alien bodies found at Roswell? And if so, where are they now?

ALIEN AUTOPSY

In 1995, an amazing movie was released to the world. The movie had been made in 1947, and showed the body of a dead alien from the Roswell crash.

In the movie, the dead, naked body is lying on a table. It has a large, round belly. Its six fingers are slightly curled. There is a deep cut in its right leg. Its twisted face seems to show pain. Two glassy eyes stare up at the ceiling.

Two doctors stand over the body. They wear white suits to protect themselves from alien infection. First they slice the creature's chest open. They remove its bloody organs. Then they saw its skull in half to look at the brain. On the outside, the creature looks a bit like a human. On the inside, it looked like nothing on Earth.

But did the movie prove that aliens exist, or was it just a hoax?

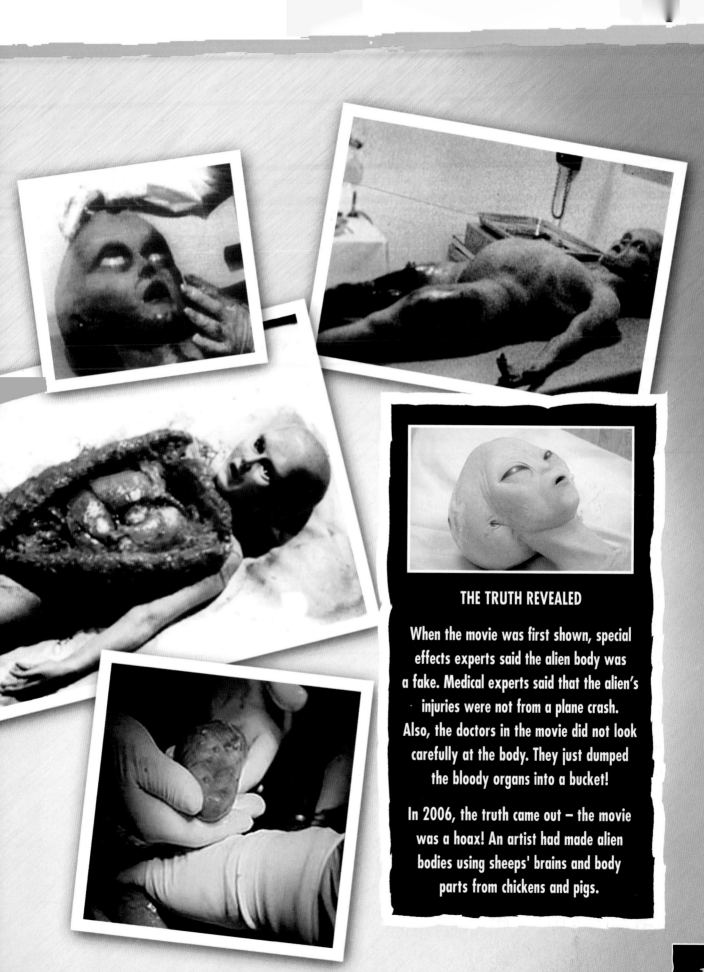

THE TRUTH REVEALED

When the movie was first shown, special effects experts said the alien body was a fake. Medical experts said that the alien's injuries were not from a plane crash. Also, the doctors in the movie did not look carefully at the body. They just dumped the bloody organs into a bucket!

In 2006, the truth came out – the movie was a hoax! An artist had made alien bodies using sheeps' brains and body parts from chickens and pigs.

HOT SPOTS

Where is the best place to find aliens? Some places in the world are UFO 'hot spots'. These are areas where UFO and alien sightings are common.

Brazil has more UFO sightings than anywhere else in the world. In 1980, the town of Tres Coroas was terrorised for 20 days by hovering UFOs.

In Russia, a remote area near the Ural Mountains is known as the M-triangle. Local people in the M-triangle describe strange lights and signs written in the sky. They have also reported meeting glowing aliens in the forest.

If you are worried about aliens, stay away from the east coast of the United States. More alien kidnaps have been reported here than anywhere else in the world!

Aliens aren't fussy about where they land. They've been seen in cities, towns, on farms and even soggy marshes.

NEW YORK ABDUCTION

Linda Napolitano from New York, USA, believed she had been abducted by aliens many times. Under hypnosis she remembered being taken out through the walls of her 12th floor apartment and up to a spaceship. Amazingly, around the same time, two police officers said they saw a woman floating over New York, towards a UFO !

THE CHUPACABRAS – GOAT SUCKERS

This terrifying group of creatures are found mainly in Puerto Rico. Chupacabras are around ¾ metre tall, have huge, red eyes, fangs and long claws. At night they attack farm animals, tearing them apart and eating them.

Some people believe they are the crew of a crashed alien spaceship. Others think they might be escaped creatures from a secret government experiment!

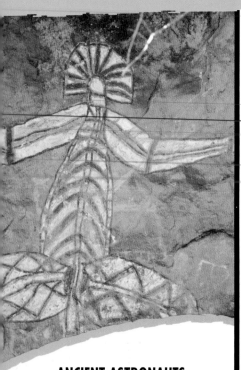

ANCIENT ASTRONAUTS

In the myths of
Australian Aborigines,
the world was created by
spirits called *Wandjina*.

These spirits came to
Earth in flying craft
from other worlds.
Wandjina paintings show
figures with halos
around their heads.
Could these halos be the
helmets from spacesuits?

ALIENS IN HISTORY

"**M**any large, black globes were seen in the air, moving before the Sun at great speed and turning against each other as if fighting. Some of them became red and fiery and afterwards faded and went out."

This UFO report is over 450 years old! It was written on 7th August, 1566, by a student living in Basel, Switzerland. Since ancient times people have reported seeing strange objects and lights in the sky, and mysterious, non-human creatures!

Around 590 BC, the prophet Ezekial took seven days to recover after seeing a "great cloud with brightness around it and fire flashing forth". He also saw four creatures with wings and legs. Could these be ancient aliens?

ALIEN MONUMENTS?

In 1969, Swiss writer Erich von Daniken claimed that alien astronauts had visited Earth. He said that they helped to build the pyramids in Egypt and Stonehenge in England. Most of his theories have now been proved wrong by historians.

ALIEN BOOKS

Many science fiction books and stories have imagined what would happen if humans and aliens met.

One of the first stories about aliens visiting Earth was *Micromegas*. It was written in the 1750s by the French writer Voltaire. Two giants come to Earth from Sirius and Saturn. They laugh at how stupid humans are!

In *Day of the Triffids* (1951) by John Wyndham, killer plants from outer space take over the world. In Douglas Adams's *Hitchhikers Guide to the Galaxy* (1979), Earth is demolished by aliens to make way for a new highway through space!

The War of the Worlds (1898) by H.G. Wells describes a Martian invasion of Earth. After landing in space-cylinders, the Martians build enormous three-legged fighting machines. They destroy everything in their path. Soon red alien weeds cover all of Earth. In the end, the Martians are defeated by a common human germ.

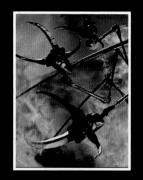

THE FIGHTING MACHINES

"They were described as 'vast spider-like machines, nearly a hundred feet high, capable of the speed of an express train, and able to shoot out a beam of intense heat.'"

A description of the Martian fighting machines in *The War of the Worlds* (1898) by H. G. Wells.

EXPLORING THE UNIVERSE

In movies and TV shows such as *Star Trek* and *Star Wars*, brave human explorers meet strange creatures.

They find many different types of aliens, all over the galaxy. Some of them are intelligent beings, or colourful clouds floating in space. Others are terrifying monsters that gobble up spaceship crews.

MOVIE ALIENS

On their way back to Earth, the crew of a spaceship visit a dead planet. But something is alive there, something terrible...

In *Alien* (1979), a hideous alien life form hitches a ride on a spaceship and gradually kills the crew members one by one. The 'Alien' went on to star in three sequels.

In the movies, aliens love to attack humans! In the very first science fiction movie, *A Trip to the Moon* (1902), exploding moon-men chase astronauts.

Many 1950's movies feature bizarre aliens, such as *The Blob* (1958). In this movie, a meteor carries a giant monster to Earth. It looks like a huge blob of raspberry jam. On Earth, it spreads out and squashes everyone who gets in its way!

IFOS

Thousands of UFOs are reported every year. People get very excited about them because they believe they are a sign that alien life is close by. However, most of the UFO sightings can be explained by weather or man-made objects.

PROJECT BLUE BOOK

In 1947, the United States government began officially researching UFOs. This became known as *Project Blue Book*. Their final report said that there was not enough evidence to carry on the study.

Some people believe that governments try to cover up UFO sightings. They claim that special, top secret agents, known as 'Men in Black', try to stop stories about aliens spreading.

Many UFO sightings are actually man-made IFOs (Identified Flying Objects). IFOs include low-flying planes, balloons and satellites. Sometimes, they are top-secret test planes.

Some IFOs are meteors. Others are clouds with a strange shape (like the one in this picture) which look like flying saucers.

It is very hard to prove a real UFO sighting, especially when pictures are fuzzy or the object appears a long way away. Many UFO photos turn out to be hoaxes or jokes, using models or trick photography.

FREAKS OF NATURE

Natural wonders such as the Aurora Borealis make weird effects in the sky. The Aurora Borealis are lights which can be seen in the sky near the Arctic Circle. They are made by natural electricity in the air.

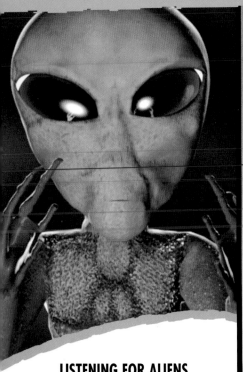

DO ALIENS EXIST?

It is hard to prove whether aliens exist. If aliens are here, they have probably been visiting us for thousands of years already. So don't panic – they haven't harmed us yet!

There may be alien life somewhere in our own solar system. We already know that the planet Venus is too hot and poisonous for life to survive. But in 2004, two robot explorers were sent to Mars where they found signs of water. Where there is water, there is usually life.

Scientists are also looking into space for other planets like our Earth that might be able to grow life. The Hubble Space Telescope has shown that there are billions of galaxies like ours. So there is a very good chance that alien life does exist!

LISTENING FOR ALIENS

Since 1971, scientists have tried to pick up radio signals sent by aliens. So far, no proof of extra terrestrial life has been found.

Scientists from the European Space Agency, Darwin project are also looking for planets that could support life. By 2015, they hope to send three space telescopes out into the universe. These telescopes will look for signs of life on other planets.

LIFE ON MARS

Mars is our nearest planet. NASA scientists believe there is a strong chance that life exists there. They think it's hidden in underground caves. These Martians won't be scary monsters, but tiny microbes.

GLOSSARY & INDEX

Abduction Taking someone away against their will. Another word for kidnap.

Astronomer A scientist who studies space.

Autopsy An examination to find out why someone, or something, died.

Crop circle A flattened pattern made in a field of crops. Some people believe crop circles are made by people playing tricks. Others think they are made by aliens in UFOs.

Extra terrestrial Something from another planet or another part of the universe.

Flying saucer An early name for UFOs. Many UFOs look like big discs or a metal saucer flying through the air.

Galaxy A large group of about 100 billion stars. Earth (which is a planet) is part of the Milky Way Galaxy.

Hypnosis When a hypnotist uses special words and actions to make someone fall into a sleep-like state. People who are hypnotised can be made to remember things they have forgotten in normal life!

Meteor a piece of rock or metal from outer space.

Microbes Tiny, simple living things.

NASA (National Aeronautics and Space Administration) An American organisation that studies space and builds spacecraft.

Satellites Spacecraft that circle the Earth sending and receiving radio and TV signals.

Sighting (UFO) An occasion when a UFO has been seen.

Solar system The nine planets, including our Earth, that circle the Sun.

UFO An Unidentified Flying Object. An object that cannot be explained by human activities or nature.

Universe Everything that exists anywhere!

Viruses Small particles that infect the cells of living things.